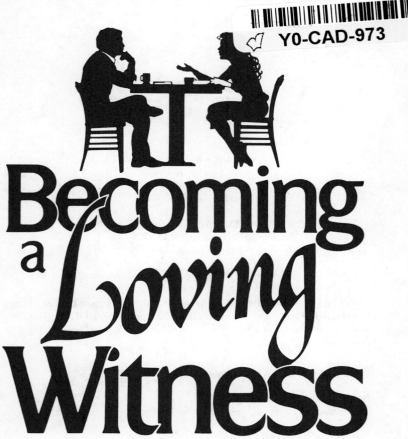

Becoming a *Loving* Witness

... to an unsaved mate

Marion Beavers

BROADMAN PRESS
Nashville, Tennessee

Dewey Decimal Classification: 248.5
Subject Heading: WITNESSING
Library of Congress Catalog Card Number: 87-15335

Printed in the United States of America

Unless otherwise indicated, all Scripture quotations are from the King James Version of the Bible. Quotations marked (NIV) are from HOLY BIBLE *New International Version,* copyright © 1978, New York Bible Society. Used by permission.

Library of Congress Cataloging-in-Publication Data

Beavers, Marion, 1914-
  Becoming a loving witness / Marion Beavers.
    p. cm.
  ISBN 0-8054-5670-8
  1. Witness bearing (Christianity)   2. Beavers, Marion, 1914-
I. Title.
BV4520.B357 1988
248'.5'0924—dc19   87-15335
                                                               CIP

To Ken
With Love

Have I been persecuting Jesus by a zealous determination to serve Him in my own way? If I feel I have done my duty and yet have hurt Him in doing it, I may be sure it was not my duty, because it has not fostered the meek and quiet spirit, but the spirit of self-satisfaction. We imagine that whatever is unpleasant is our duty! Is that anything like the spirit of our Lord—"I *delight* to do Thy will, O My God"?

From *My Utmost for His Highest,* The Golden Book of Oswald Chambers (New York: Dodd, Mead & Company, Inc., n.d.), p. 29.

Contents

Contents

Introduction

"I am not ashamed of the gospel of Christ: for it is the power of God unto salvation to every one that believeth" (Rom. 1:16).

These were the words of the famed and beloved apostle Paul as he wrote to the Christians in Rome on his journey from Ephesus to Greece. Peter was not ashamed of the gospel of Christ when he stood before thousands in Jerusalem at Pentecost and boldly witnessed to the power of the risen Lord. Stephen was not ashamed of the gospel of Christ as he was being stoned by his enemies, holding on to his faith to the very end.

Witnessing is the very essence of the life of a Christian. It is second nature to one who has been born into the kingdom of God by accepting Christ as Lord and Savior of his or her life. The desire comes suddenly. The boldness is there. We want to tell everyone about Jesus, and we especially long to win over the non-Christian to this wonderful new life.

Most of us, however, fail to use caution and insight at first. We rush into our new "calling" with a zeal which can often negate any change which we hope to effect in the lives of our chosen recipients. We are not winsome in our witness.

This story was written to show the disastrous effect in my own life of overzealousness and the importance of presenting a proper witness to our non-Christian friends and families.

None of us, as Christians, are ashamed of the gospel of Jesus Christ. But let us give Christ His due and His glory by planting the seeds His way, not ours.

1

O Happy Day

"What is happening to us?" I said aloud as I stood numbly by the kitchen door, waiting for my husband to join me. Ken and I had an appointment with a marriage counselor, and this was difficult for me even to envision. Three months ago I was glowing with joy, secure in the knowledge that I had given my life to Christ, and was, therefore, in the family of God. I would also have eternal life, a promise from the third chapter of the Book of John in the Bible. The sixteenth verse says, "For God so loved the world, that he gave his only begotten Son, that whosoever believeth in him should not perish, but have everlasting life." I believed and gratefully cherished this verse and its promise.

Ken was my college sweetheart. After a three-year courtship, we parted, due mainly to the financial pressures of Depression years and Ken's consequent inability to afford the expenses of marriage. He maintained the old-fashioned idea that he wanted to be the sole breadwinner of the family, and his first job out of college barely kept his own body and soul together. Taking a wife would be impossible—to him. Unfortunately, he did not share this with me; but, wanting me to have the opportunity to marry someone else, he led me to believe he had other interests, although this was not the case. I was terribly hurt by his "rejection" and carried the so-called "torch" for several years. Then I met Jule, the man I was to marry.

This first marriage was a happy one, and Jule and I were blessed with two precious children, a girl and a boy. But the marriage was to last only seventeen years. Jule died of a sudden heart attack in the prime of his life, and I was left a grief-stricken widow.

Two and a half years later, I surprisingly met Ken again at the home of mutual college friends who lived in the same city where I resided. Since his marriage had also ended tragically, we began seeing each other whenever he came to my locale, a distance of over two hundred miles. The strong attraction returned, and within about eight months, we were married. My sixteen-year-old daughter was my maid of honor, and she and my thirteen-year-old son were pleased that they once more had a father. But all was not roses.

This second marriage was off to a shaky beginning because of teenage problems and a husband who drank heavily—something of which I was unaware before Ken and I married. I assumed he was the same person I had known years before, not considering that we all change with time and circumstances. Then my mother succumbed to cancer, and my father had serious surgery, necessitating constant care on my part. I was drained physically and emotionally.

One evening, with Ken "passed out" on the couch and my father retired for the night, I got in my car trying to escape and find someone with whom to share my problems. I needed a listening ear. At the age of fifty-six, my life had been in intense turmoil for over a decade; and finally I felt I had reached the saturation point. As I drove down a neighboring street, a strong but inaudible Voice said, "Don't go, Marion!"

I reacted like Jacob of old, as he wrestled with the angel, and protested, "But I want to. . . ."

Again the Voice, and again my stubborn answer. Finally I pulled over to the curb, wondering just what was happening.

Once more the Voice, urging me to return home. This time I obeyed.

All was quiet when I went into the house. My husband and father were still asleep, and obviously I had not been missed. My problems were still there—like dark shadows waiting to pounce on me —but I resignedly went to bed, expecting another night of tossing and turning. Instead, I slept like a baby.

Sunday morning when I awoke, I went into the

kitchen and looked out the window. Everything
was serene, beautiful, and lovely—more so to me
than ever before—and I was suffused with a peace
and joy beyond my understanding. I knew my
problems were still there. I knew nothing around
me had changed. But somehow I had changed inwardly. At that moment, I was on top of the world,
and I could not comprehend it.

I was the only family member planning to attend
church that morning. I usually attended because it
was a lifelong habit and "obligation" which I en-
joyed. I was active in the church, had taken the
children to Sunday School and church, and had
even taught Sunday School myself. However, I
knew nothing about a personal commitment to
Christ, and I rarely read the Bible with its small
print and difficult passages. I did know for some
reason that this particular Sunday was special for
me.

Sunday School was still going on as I walked into
the schoolhouse church, so I sat down and quietly
waited. A visitor later came up to me and said,
"You looked positively radiant when you walked in
that door!"

"I don't know why," I replied, "because my
whole world is falling apart."

"Then I know what has happened to you," he
answered.

Right at that instant, the letters H-O-L-Y S-P-I-R-
I-T seemed to etch themselves on my brain, as

from a teletype machine. That is the only way I can describe it; and then I knew. God, in His unspeakable grace, had reached down and touched this sinner when I needed Him most.

Our young pastor gave his first altar call, and nothing could have prevented me from all but running down the aisle, eyes brimming with tears, and giving my life to Jesus Christ, asking Him to be my Lord and Savior. I can never forget the love which filled my soul as God's Holy Spirit performed His work. I was a new creation.

Since my life now had added spiritual dimensions, I was filled with heaven-sent awe and immense gratitude. I believe this must be the reaction of all newly born-again Christians. The Creator of the entire universe had touched me and given me an inner peace and joy which could not possibly be described. He had welcomed me into His family as an adopted daughter. I knew personally what kind of love that entailed, since I was the parent of an adopted daughter myself. I now knew the real meaning of that wonderful and familiar song:

> Jesus loves me! this I know,
> For the Bible tells me so;
> Little ones to him belong;
> They are weak, but he is strong.

> Yes, Jesus loves me,

Yes, Jesus loves me,
Yes, Jesus loves me,
The Bible tells me so.

ANNA B. WARNER

I also knew the meaning of Paul's words in Ephesians 2:8-9: "For by grace are ye saved through faith; and that not of yourselves: it is the gift of God: Not of works, lest any man should boast." There was no merit in me. My "Damascus-road" experience had not even been sought. I felt special, but very humble indeed.

I had taken the turn in my life which was the ultimate decision that God wills for each person on earth. The Bible is full of Scriptures which point to a person's making this decision.

After His resurrection and just before His ascension unto the Father, Jesus said, "Go ye into all the world, and preach the gospel to every creature" (Mark 16:15).

It was His earnest wish and plan that every living being would hear about and accept Him as Lord of their lives. I am thankful to God daily I took that important spiritual step.

But little did I know this would be the beginning of a long series of problems, testing my faith and taking me to the point of threatened divorce.

2

Coming on Strong

Days after my conversion, the joy was still present as I continued to float on some remote cloud of rapture. I had been a Christian for *almost a whole week,* and now I wanted everyone to know Jesus Christ as I did, especially my family and close friends. How exciting it was to consider their positive responses and eternal gratitude for what I had to tell them. My neighborhood Christian book store began to flourish from the first day I paid it a visit.

"Please show me all the books you have for a brand-new Christian to read," I asked the owner of the small but only Christian book store in town. "I have just accepted Christ and can hardly wait to read some good material about the Christian life!"

"Praise the Lord!" he exclaimed, and immediately went to his shelves and produced a number of books such as *A Taste of New Wine* by Keith Miller, *Under New Management* by Sam Shoemaker, and a few others which were testimonies of

such well-known Christians as Dale Evans and Roy
Rogers. I eagerly browsed around and also found a
number of pamphlets and booklets; by the time I
finished looking, I added considerably to his till; to
say nothing of my anticipation of reading every
word of every book and pamphlet. Our checking
account gravitated, but my spirits soared.

Another thought came to me. *My family! These
books would help them, too! I knew absolutely that
Ken would be terribly interested in Roy Rogers's
testimony, for he simply loved Western stories.
And who was more Western than Roy Rogers?
Maybe, just maybe, Ken would find what I had
found. And we could share it together, and his
whole life would change. It was going to be wonderful!* My thoughts tumbled into every conceiva-
ble direction, scattered by excitement and hope.

There was our son, David, and his wife Loraine.
They were not Christians and also needed to know
about the Christian life. I would take them *Under
New Management.* Surely they would seriously
consider its words of wisdom. I understood it per-
fectly and thought it inspiring. It might be the
beginning of a new life for David and Loraine. Oh,
how I hoped so!

Then there was our daughter, Susan. She lived in
another city with her husband and small baby, and
they had joined a church which was rather un-
familiar to me. It sounded good, they preached
good morals and clean living and doing good

works, but I wasn't sure that they knew about a personal relationship with Jesus Christ. I could send them *A Taste of New Wine.*

So I packaged up the book for Susan and Sam and dropped it into the mail with a fervent prayer and a feeling of confidence that this would plant the necessary seed in their minds. Then I drove out to see David and Loraine and tenderly handed them the book which I hoped would greatly affect their lives.

My prime target was Ken. I was going to change that man! Not only did I give him the book about Roy Rogers, but I saw that pamphlets, booklets, and tracts were strategically placed around the house in accessible places where they could be picked up randomly and read with growing interest. I made certain that some were prominently arrayed on his bedside table, on the kitchen table, on the top of the commode in the bathroom, and, of course, on occasional tables in the living room. There was no way he could fail to notice some of them.

My enthusiasm and zeal for the Lord soared to new heights. There is nothing wrong with that, but the new Christian needs to take account of her every move from the viewpoint of the non-Christian. It is wise to look back in retrospect on the days before the spiritual change took place and consider one's own reaction to such enthusiasm and zeal.

I often recall the days when I attended church,

Sunday School, and a women's circle in another city and how I often scoffed inwardly at the women who were so obviously tuned in to God. I considered myself a Christian, but I thought these women were plain sanctimonious; and I did not allow myself to become close friends with them. What gems of joy and wisdom I missed by not allowing myself to share in what they had. But, of course, I did not know Jesus and could not understand those "fanatics," as I considered them.

Bible reading and Bible study became an obsession with me now. I went weekly to a ladies' share group and a church Bible study, gleaning all the knowledge I could of the Word of God. I read dozens of Christian books telling the experiences and insights of other Christians. There was no fault to find with that, with one exception. I failed to keep my priorities straight in the eyes of God. He comes first, of course; but Scripture tells us that our mates come next, before everything else, even attending Bible studies. I thought that attending Bible study groups was putting God first, but I learned the hard way that this was not so. I will enlarge on this later.

I began to quote the Bible to family and friends, and this, too, is acceptable in its place. However, it can be overdone; and finally one of my closest friends had to enlighten me. She was a non-Christian and was talking on the subject of remarrying after the death of one's mate. I very forcefully informed her of the biblical stand on the matter, and she replied with equal force, "You turn me off. You have your religion, and I have mine. Now let's not talk about it anymore!"

To this day, we have not been able to discuss our faith together; and I feel certain that it is partly because I was not winsome in my witness. If the word *winsome* is divided it tells you something. When one is winsome, one may "win some." If one is overzealous like I was, one may, in all probability, "oversell" and "lose some." I doubt that my friend liked the change in my life, simply because she did not see the inner change I wanted her to see.

C. T. Studd once said, "It is as essential to be Christian in our attitudes toward one another as it is to be orthodox in our faith." I was developing the wrong attitude, even though with the best of intentions. I was coming on too strong with what I called my Christian witness. I wanted to save everyone around me from a burning hell. Of course, I still do; but my attitude has, thankfully, changed. The Holy Spirit is the One who changes a person and draws him or her to Christ. The Christian can plant seeds in that person, but all the persuasion in the world will not help without the leading of the Holy Spirit.

A. W. Tozer stated it well, "I wouldn't ever try to push one of God's children into any knowledge or any experience, because I have found that we try to push too much and too soon. We only result in kicking God's children out of their shells too soon, and as a result, we have a lot of weird monstrosities instead of saints. I don't want to do that!"[1]

At that time in my life, I was completely unaware of this wisdom.

3

Two Different Worlds

"Why won't you come to Bible study with me tonight?" I asked Ken one Sunday evening. "Other men go with their wives, and I know you'd enjoy it."

"I don't want to go," he retorted. "I want to stay home tonight. You go ahead and go if you want to."

"Well, I always seem to be the one who goes alone without her husband. I feel like a fifth wheel!"

"You don't want me to go if I don't want to go, do you?" he questioned me, looking me straight in the eyes.

"Well, no, but I can't see why you wouldn't want to go and learn something more about the Bible. It's better than that TV you watch." I could assert that with sincerity.

"Just go ahead and go, Honey. I really don't mind, and I know you enjoy it. I simply want to stay home," he answered with finality.

So I went, and continued to attend every Sunday

evening for well over a year. I also joined a Monday-morning breakfast group, which met at the church at 6:30. We took turns bringing breakfast for the others, and I felt good about getting home by 8:30 to fix Ken's breakfast, even if he arose at seven. On Tuesdays, I met with a "share group," as it was called, and I always made certain to arrive back in time to throw a lunch together for Ken when he came home. It wasn't long, however, before he began eating with the other men at work each day, and I wondered why he preferred to spend three dollars daily on lunch rather than come home for the homemade sandwich I would give him—usually a piece of cold cut or cheese between two slices of bread.

Life for me was a series of Bible studies and church meetings, for by then I was chairing committees, teaching Sunday School, and taking on some rather large projects. Organizing was my "thing," and now I could do it for the Lord. Ken never said a word when I attended a "discipline-and-discovery" group at least two evenings a week. And I did not feel badly, because I was now putting God first in my life, or so I thought.

Then there was the weekend retreat as the "discipline-and-discovery" program ended. It was extremely uplifting, and I came home on a spiritual "high."

My next step in growing in the Lord was to join a lay witness mission, which involved a group of

Christians going to another town and witnessing all weekend at one of the local churches. This is one of the most fulfilling things a Christian can do; and, once more, I came home on a spiritual mountaintop. I had been chosen to give my testimony at a women's luncheon. Although I was so frightened in front of the large group of strangers that I had to grab a napkin and pull on it as I talked, I was sincere in my desire to do this for the Lord.

What did Ken do all of these times I was away from home? I know now that he went to the bottle more and more for "companionship," but he never spoke a word to me about wanting me to stay home. I actually thought he didn't care, but no man could have displayed more patience.

Soon an exciting thing happened. A well-known evangelist was coming to town for a city-wide crusade, and I found myself right in the middle of the planning. I divided up the city on a map and delegated all the churches to various people to contact, seeking to involve them in the crusade. In addition to that, I took a week-long course in counseling from two men who were top trainers. This was another splendid spiritual experience for me, and my minister gave me his undivided support.

And what was Ken doing all those evenings I was training to be a counselor for the Lord? He uncomplainingly stayed home, nursing his bottle of bourbon when he became bored or lonesome. Of course, I never considered this, since I was "putting God first" in my life. Surely my example would eventually rub off on him. Certainly he would see the change in my life and want to change his life also. *It was inevitable,* I reflected.

I obtained Ken's promise that he would attend the crusade at least one night. I just knew that if he came at least once and heard the inspiring messages and saw the juggling act and other added attractions, he would want to come back. Well, he attended one night, and that was it. I craned my neck looking for him after the altar call was given, but he did not show up in the counseling room. I had retained high hopes that this would happen, but my hopes were shattered.

"Didn't you just love the crusade?" I asked him joyfully on the way home. I had experienced a seemingly satisfactory counseling session with a mixed-up young man, and I was glowing with the apparent results.

"It was OK," he answered stiffly. "But I never did go for that mass going-forward business," he added. "Most of those people are counselors anyway."

"That's not true!" I protested. "There were other people in the counseling room. Why do you have to be that way?"

"Because I am," he stated flatly, and the conversation ended.

I was glum because things did not turn out like I wanted, and Ken was obviously dissatisfied with the whole evening. He had a "thing" about crusades, and years later I found out why. He associated them with tent meetings, and he had undergone a bad experience with a charlatan at a series of tent meetings before we married. The man had "healed" dozens of people and told them to throw down their crutches and braces. Since Ken worked for a rehabilitation service, they would come to him the next day, beseeching his help in getting new prostheses, since they had not been healed at all. His confidence in crusades or tent meetings had been badly shaken, though wrongly so in the present case.

My resentment was building. I was doing everything I knew for God, who had changed my life and had given me the ability to live with my problems. Now my husband was presenting me with a new problem. *Instead of entering into my newfound joy and way of life, he is stubbornly holding onto his old ways and causing a wall to come between us,* so I thought.

However, I kept on optimistically leaving tracts and books around, and they sat as untouched as a cold dish of oatmeal. Instead, he avidly read *Reader's Digest, National Geographic,* paperback Westerns, and spy stories. *What was the matter with him?* I thought to myself. *Everything he reads is secular literature, if, in fact, the Westerns and spy stories could be called literature!*

My busy church life continued at such a pace

that our times together were becoming less and less frequent. When Ken and I did sit down to talk, our communication was lacking. "Hmmm" became a common but overworked sound.

"Where is your faith?" I would ask desperately.

"I have a deep faith," he would answer simply but with conviction.

"Please tell me about it," I would entreat.

"It's very personal to me. It's something I can't talk about."

And the matter was closed.

I began to wonder why I married this man. We had so little in common anymore!

4

Headed Toward the Rocks

Every brand-new Christian should be told by his or her pastor, as well as by other seasoned Christians, that there will be attacks by Satan. These attacks are not usually recognizable as coming from "the prince of this world." They subtly creep into the minds and lives of the new believer in the form of doubt, discouragement, reluctance to study the Bible, lack of a desire to pray, irritability, depression, or other negative characteristics. When this happens, and the Christian is aware of the source of the problem, the victim can rebuke Satan in the name of Jesus and quote a verse of Scripture to suit the problem. The attack will—as far as I have ever been able to ascertain—go away.

Jesus used this method when tempted in the wilderness just before His ministry began, and it is an excellent example for us to follow at any time in our Christian walk.

Satan chose the time of these beginning problems to bring down an onslaught on me in the guise of dissatisfaction with my marriage. Not being sufficiently enlightened about the wiles of the fallen angel, I blamed all of my feelings on my unsuspecting Ken. I was sure by then that the love we once knew had dissipated—gone away—and my vulnerable mind was playing strange tricks.

I did not have to search my memory too hard to drag forth all the previous difficulties we had encountered as a newly married couple with two teenagers and rehash these difficulties as evidence of a failing marriage. When various situations had left a scar on my mind, I now blamed Ken personally for insensitivity and poor handling, familial malpractice of sorts. Even though I may have been correct in some instances, I failed to recognize that Ken had suffered from them as much as I—even though he had done the things which seemed right at the particular times in question. To hand a man two teenagers as a wedding gift is no small matter to comprehend!

Gradually I began to confront my bewildered husband with all of these grudges I had obviously been putting on hold in the back of my mind. I was daily quenching the Holy Spirit with my attitude and accusations. And the more I did this, the easier it became. My heart was becoming hardened. Satan was having a heyday with me, and I fell right into his trap.

Meanwhile, Ken became more and more distracted as I looked upon him as a non-Christian;

and I could see him rebelling at the standards I set up for him. He continued to drink heavily and to withdraw into himself. His bright, inherent sense of humor faded when I was around, but I noticed he was friendly and jovial around others. Yet, he never openly criticized me or showed me lack of respect. I could appreciate that much, at least.

Since my elderly father lived with us, we lacked the privacy we really needed to work out these growing problems. Fortunately, I had a truly wonderful dad; and although he must have been acutely aware of the hostility in our midst, he never questioned me about it. He stayed much in his own section of the home and spent a great deal of his time with a dear little neighbor lady, thus saving embarrassment on his part and mine. And Ken's!

I frantically sought counseling—alone.

"You have every reason to seek a divorce," one counselor advised me. "But do you really want it?"

"I don't like the idea," I replied. "But how can I go on living like this?"

Then we would pray, and I would leave for another week.

One day I heard of a different counselor who was supposedly helping a friend of mine. He was a retired minister, and I considered that sufficient qualification.

I drove out to his house, almost dreading to go over the whole story again, but he welcomed me warmly and listened to my (by now) well-rehearsed speech. Then he said something which shocked me into never going to see him again.

"Have you ever considered having an affair with someone?" he asked.

"An aff . . . fair?" I sputtered.

"Exactly," he answered. "It is often good therapy."

I cannot recall any further conversation between us, for I was all too anxious to get out of there. I left that counselor and returned to the original one, a truly godly man who tried his best to help me. Finally, he acknowledged he had done all he could. The rest was up to me, since his suggestion of counseling both of us was met by Ken with a decisive "No!"

After much persuasion on my part, I finally convinced Ken to seek out an entirely new counselor, one who was not a pastor. Ken is of high intellect and felt that a professional counseling firm was the only recourse for us, if counseling were indeed the last resort. I personally thought that it was.

Our pastor recommended a firm which appeared to be secular in nature. I could tell that Ken was going to our first session grudgingly and surmised that it was because he had done counseling himself in the past, and a piece of his pride was being chopped away because he was going to someone else for his problems.

Now we were ready to leave and seek professional help from this man. The impact of it all bore down heavily upon me as I waited for Ken by the kitchen door.

We drove silently to the counselor's office as if we were being placed on trial. Strictly speaking, we were.

The man was genial and seemed to relate very well with Ken right away. This pleased me, of course, except that I wondered whose "side" he would be on. Naturally, I secretly hoped he would be on mine. I was certain he would when he heard my story. I desired his sympathy.

He first asked me to tell him about our problem, and I laid it out long and strong, leaving out very little. When he asked Ken to give his side of the story, Ken spoke sparingly and said nothing against me. This shocked me, and I found that it heaped coals of fire on my head. It had the desired effect of the Scripture which says: "Therefore if thine enemy hunger, feed him; if he thirst, give him drink: for in so doing thou shalt heap coals of fire on his head" (Rom. 12:20); or "Love your enemies, bless them that curse you" (Matt. 5:44).

"Now I want each of you to think for a moment and give me your definition of the word *love*," he said. He first turned to Ken for an answer.

"Love is an emotion, a feeling," said my husband.

When the counselor turned to me, my mind raced to the famous love chapter in 1 Corinthians and I mumbled something about, "Love is not puffed up." And I wondered why the man looked at me strangely! No one could have been more "puffed up" than I was.

Finally we were given a question-and-answer sheet to fill in containing questions about ourselves. An evaluation of these would be given to us at the next session. Then we left, with instructions to make it a point to have at least one fancy dinner at home, by candlelight, with no one else present. Dad would be no problem, since he had gone on a trip.

The week went by with very little change, in spite of the special dinner. I had set the table with our good china, crystal, and silver. I had prepared a good meal, and we ate by candlelight. It was fairly pleasant, but the joy was missing.

At our next session with the counselor, I could hardly wait for the excellent evaluation he would give me and for his sympathy concerning my home situation. What a surprise I was in for! As it turned out, Ken received the best evaluation, and I was told some things I had never before heard about myself. Most of these were not relevant to the situation, but I began to sense the fact that he considered me as part of the problem, me—a born-again Christian!

Finally, after the four agreed-upon sessions, he reluctantly told us that he saw little hope for our making a go of our marriage. However, he wanted each of us to come back one more time separately. Ken refused, saying he had carried out his part of the agreement—which was true. The very fact that he went at all was more than I would have ever hoped. So I agreed to return myself.

In the meantime, I made an appointment to see our lawyer, certain our marriage was over and acknowledging the fact that the Christian walk was not an easy one.

5

A Sunbeam,
Not an Atomic Blast

"I can't sleep with a woman who shows no love for me," announced Ken one evening, flinging his pajamas and bathrobe over one arm and heading out the bedroom door.

"What do you intend to do?" I questioned with an expressionless voice and face.

"I'll sleep on the couch in the living room. It opens out into a bed, you know," he answered sharply, leaving the bedroom.

We had an extra room he could have used, but it backed up to Dad's. With Ken sleeping in the living room, our privacy was more assured. We reasoned that Dad need not know how far our differences had gone, but we did not give that kindly and wise old gentleman credit for the perception he had.

I don't know how well Ken slept, since I never did ask him; but I do know that my nights were spent tossing and turning feverishly. Ken looked ten years older, and his nerves were at the snapping point. He continually balled his fingers into a fist, and his eyes held a faraway look. All closeness between us was gone.

I did not reveal to Ken that I had made an appointment with the lawyer, since he had reacted so severely about going to see a counselor. I also thought I would wait and see what the lawyer said.

When the day of my appointment came, I was nervous and depressed. A Bible lay on his large oak desk, facing me as I sat opposite him, a reminder to me that God does not look upon divorce lightly. I knew I must choose my words carefully.

"Well, Marion, what brings you here?" the very pleasant middle-aged man asked.

"I want to talk with you about a divorce," I replied, hardly believing my own ears.

"A divorce?" he exclaimed in a surprised voice, having known us as a family for quite some time.

"Yes, Mr. Palmer, things have not been going well lately." And I once more went through the story I had told three times before.

After asking me about counseling and other alternatives, he finally said he could make the necessary arrangements if and when I desired. I gave him no final go-ahead but said that I would call him. I needed more time to think, for so much would be involved.

There would be the home. Who would remain in it? I had no income of my own to go elsewhere, and of course I would need to take Dad with me if I left.

I did not have the heart to ask Ken to leave, because I knew how much he loved the place. It had been our dream home. My father needed a place where a wheelchair could be used, and there were few such houses or apartments available in our town. If Ken left, I would feel guilty about his having to spend the extra money on keeping up two places. I could not go to work because I had the care of Dad. These were all things I had not previously considered, and now they became mountains to be moved. I wondered what God wanted me to do. Suddenly I felt completely helpless.

The day soon arrived when I was due to see the marriage counselor one more time—by myself. I held little hope for the outcome of our meeting, but I got ready and was just about to go out the kitchen door to my car when something stopped me.

"Stay with Ken, and I will make you happy," said a very clear but inaudible Voice, the same Voice I had heard the night before I gave my life over to Jesus.

Somehow it did not surprise me this time. I accepted it as coming from the great I AM, the Triune God who watches over and promises to care for His own. Once more He had let me reach a point where only He could help me before He stepped in with His grace and gave me the clear direction He wanted me to take. How great and kind and loving He is!

A beautiful peace suddenly washed over and through me, and I knew now what I was to do. I was to take Him at His word and do exactly as He asked. I was through fretting, through questioning, through looking to people for answers. I need shed no more tears concerning my marriage, for His Word is true and good. In spite of the circumstances, I could believe Him for that.

Hastening to my car, I drove to the counselor's office and excitedly waited fifteen minutes for him. When he finally invited me into his office, I could hardly maintain my composure as I told him exactly what had happened, wondering if he would actually believe me.

"Here I have been working for fifteen minutes trying to work out another possible help for you, and you don't even need me any more. You have it all put together!" he exclaimed joyfully. "You see, I'm a minister, so I understand what you are saying," he added.

"A minister?" I questioned. "But we thought we were coming to a secular counselor. You never said you were a minister."

"I rarely do, but my credentials are on the walls of my office. I find it is often more helpful if I don't advertise the fact."

The peace and joy had now returned to my life, and I truly looked forward to Ken's coming home from work that evening. Even the birds sounded sweeter that day, and the flowers were surely more

beautiful. I prepared a nice dinner and waited im-
patiently for Ken to drive up.

Ken arrived at the usual time, and he barely
spoke as he came into the house, poured himself a
drink, and went out on the patio to relax. I fol-
lowed him.

"Ken, I have something to tell you," I said shyly,
not certain of what his reaction would be to the
new turn of events.

As I stood beside him, I almost feared telling him
my news. *After all, he might have changed his
mind about me,* I considered. Lately I had given
him very little reason to cherish me.

"What is it?" he asked somberly, as if expecting
the worst. Good news had been scarce for a long
time.

"I've decided to accept you just as you are, and
I want us to start all over again, putting the past
behind us as if it had never happened. Would you
agree to that?"

"Oh, Honey," he said, letting out a long breath
and setting down his drink. "Do you really mean
it?"

"Yes, I do," I assured him. "I mean it very
much."

Ken pulled me down beside him and gently took
me in his arms, holding me for a long time without
saying a word. I could almost feel the tension leaving him, just as if he were shedding the heavy
mantle of anxiety. I had shed my mantle hours

before, and now we were both free, free in the liberty only God can give.

I told him the story of what had happened, and I further shared that I knew now I was an intrinsic part of our problem. I had mentally elevated my own spirituality to the place where I had become a Pharisee in my attitude toward him and others. I was judging him, whereas Jesus said, "Judge not, that ye be not judged" (Matt. 7:1). I had failed to see that each person—including Ken—comes to the Father in different expressions of emotion and personality; and the Spirit is the One who draws the individual, not another person. Had I only known it, Ken did have a relationship with God, but it had been quenched considerably by the loss through divorce of his two children.

Our troubles were not over. They are never over for anyone in this life, even the Christian. But I knew we could rise above them now. God was with us, and "If God be for us, who can be against us?" (Rom. 8:31).

What a thrilling challenge we had ahead of us now! God was faithful to His Word. We have been, and still are, happy. Our "houses" had to be cleaned, but that has been a wonderful part of growing in Him.

> 'Tis so sweet to trust in Jesus,
>   Just to take him at his word;
>   Just to rest upon his promise,

Just to know "Thus saith the Lord."

Jesus, Jesus, how I trust him!
How I've proved him o're and o're!
Jesus, Jesus, precious Jesus!
O for grace to trust him more!

LOUISA M. R. STEAD

6

Looking Back

Sam Shoemaker wisely said, "What has often passed for 'witness' in the past is shopworn and outmoded today. You cannot tackle people with an abrupt inquiry into the state of their souls' health. You cannot quote Scripture to them right off, without preliminaries. Most evangelical lingo is both incomprehensible and distasteful to modern people. A simpler, more natural, and truly unprofessional approach is needed."[1]

The long-used but often misused verbage of the hard-hitting "Are you saved?" confrontation by a new acquaintance or absolute stranger is no longer —or rarely—effective in today's society. Nor is the question, "Are you born again?"

Dr. James Kennedy, senior minister of the Coral Ridge Presbyterian Church in Fort Lauderdale, Florida, began what is known now as Evangelism Explosion International in the 1960s. It is essentially an organized witnessing approach, usually done in teams of two or more people, and has been tre-

mendously effective. The witnesses are trained
very carefully over a period of weeks or even
months. They practice on one another and are re-
quired to witness to the whole group before ever
going out to see a single person or family. Scripture
is memorized and used, for the whole approach is
based upon the personal testimony of the witness,
along with the use of Scripture—always in context.
It is not a hard-sell encounter, and its effectiveness
has been continually proven. In Dr. Kennedy's
church alone, a congregation of 6,500 members
was built out of a group of forty-five prospects.
Thousands of churches now use this witnessing tool
and are greatly blessed. It is far from the strong,
overzealous tactic I used as a brand-new Christian.

I had met Christ. I had a real conversion experience, and I had something to share with others.
But I was not "walking in their shoes." I was not
empathizing with them, and I was certainly not
being a loving witness.

Good manners were not even a part of my witness. It is just as important to show good manners
to one's mate and be sensitive to his or her feelings
as it is to be sensitive to the feelings of those outside
the home. This is especially true in witnessing. Re-
straint is better than unleashing a barrage of words
which could frighten others or cause them to withdraw. If I had sat down with Ken, joyfully but gently sharing my experience, and then telling him
only what had happened in my own life, I believe

he would have sought rather than fought the literature and Bible study crusade which I tried to thrust
upon him.

Hindsight leads me to say this because of something which occurred in later years. My regular
Bible study phased out for various reasons, and I
hungered for another one. Finally, a group of close
friends of ours decided to meet as a couples group,
and I was overjoyed when Ken agreed to attend on
a "trial" basis. We went several times, enjoying the
fellowship of our friends. But something went
wrong with the group, and Ken was relieved that
it dissolved. I asked him to join another couples'
study with me, but he showed no interest; and I
knew by then not to beg or plead.

About that time, an advertisement appeared on
television and in magazines, describing a home
Bible study presented by a well-known Christian
college. The idea began to crystallize in my mind
that I could have my own Bible study and stay
home with Ken at the same time. The prospect was
exciting; and after talking it over with him, I en-
rolled in the course—the same course which was
given at the college itself.

The day the boxes of study materials arrived
found me eager to begin the study, which would
last over a period of two years. Not wanting to
bother Ken in any way, I had chosen a quiet and
unobtrusive place in our home to listen to the
tapes, take notes, and follow the written outlines

and Bible references. In a far corner of our sun porch, I began to play the first tape; and as the pleasant but assertive voice of the speaker introduced the course, someone sat down beside me. Yes, it was Ken. He not only listened to the first tape, which was all I had planned to play that first evening, but he said, "Let's play the next tape!" as soon as that one ended.

Thus began an intensive Bible study for both of us, and I felt a miracle had taken place. I had to study for and take the examinations, but Ken willingly helped me prepare for them by asking me long lists of study questions provided in the course.

We found ourselves discussing spiritual, archaeological, and historical matters, and this spiritual endeavor was becoming a common bond between us. Before my graduation we even ended up journeying to the Holy Land with a group of the students and professors, and few things have stirred us so deeply. Later, Ken proudly drove me to the college in another state for my graduation and took pictures of me in my cap and gown as I marched with others to receive my diploma.

The diploma meant more than passing the course for me. It represented the beginning of a spiritual journey for Ken and me which has grown steadily over the years. It said so much to me as I compared it with my immature efforts when I first became a Christian and knew so little about God. In this case, I let God touch Ken's heart in His own way. I did not have to deny or waver in my faith. I held fast to it but did not shove. The result was a shower of blessings for both of us.

Another lesson I have learned is humility. Self-righteousness has no place in the life of the Christian. Jesus condemned the scribes and Pharisees for their self-righteousness: "Woe unto you, scribes and Pharisees, hypocrites! for ye are like unto whited sepulchres, which indeed appear beautiful outward, but are within full of dead men's bones, and of all uncleanness" (Matt. 23:27).

God's Word further tells us, "There is none righteous, no not one" (Rom. 3:10). If you're a Christian, you'll know it and you'll show it. You'll show it by the love and compassion you extend to others, thus enabling them to see more of Christ in you than by any show of pride.

Sam Shoemaker also wrote, "Gratitude is the best offset to pride, and the surest source of true humility." Jesus said, "Blessed are the poor in spirit: for theirs in the kingdom of heaven" (Matt. 5:3). These are the humble, the people who give God all the glory.

Some people are so filled with self-righteousness that others truly dread seeing them come up the walk to the door. One can rightfully predict that those Pharisees will tell of their latest good works and how grateful they are that they can do all of those "good things." There is nothing wrong with their acts of kindness. Their attitude is found wanting. It is as though they want *our* praise and admiration, and so often we want to tell them that God is the only One to please. The joy comes from serving Him through kindness to others. Jesus tells us that we do serve Him when we serve others: "Verily I say unto you, Inasmuch as ye have done it unto one of the least of these my brethren, ye have done it unto me" (Matt. 25:40).

Colleen Townsend Evans has rightly said, "Happy is the woman who knows that without God she is nothing . . . but that with God working through her, she has the strength and power of His love."[3]

My self-righteous attitude toward Ken was inexcusable in God's eyes. All I had received from God was a pure gift on His part. I earned none of it and had no reason to feel pride or superiority.

As Christians, we are all given spiritual gifts; and many of us do not know for awhile what our gifts are. But each gift is a necessary part of the body of Christ—the church—and it would not do for all of us to receive the same gift. The brand-new Christian is usually unaware of this phenomenon and is easily "put down" by another who boasts of his or her gift or gifts. The opposite can also be true. If the new Christian receives a spiritual gift and recognizes it, it is likewise possible for him or her to frighten or turn away the non-Christian by its misuse or by an attitude of pride. We are to use our gifts, but we should be careful not to misuse them.

The new Christian is especially apt to do so out of overzealousness.

Hindsight again has taught me the importance of priorities according to God's standards. Even after Ken and I became reconciled, I did not change my heavy schedule of church activities. I continued to feel that this was putting God first in my life, and He was my first priority. But somehow I was confusing the person of Christ—God incarnate—with the church itself. It is one thing to put Him first in our day, in our hearts, and in our actions, but it is another thing to spend so much time in church work that we fail to see what we are doing to our homelife.

On one occasion, I heard Ken say, "My wife opens and closes the church doors." It may have sounded like a joke to the other person, but that rang a bell in my head. I knew he was saying in jest something he felt deeply, and I realized I must do something about it.

God began to deal with me, and I set my mind on the Scriptures. In reading Paul's Epistles, I realized that my priorities were all wrong. As a result, I began staying home with Ken more instead of attending every meeting and Bible study I could squeeze in. I confided these things to my pastor, and he replied in all seriousness, "Marion, you are right. Your husband must come before your church activities." God established the family before He established the church.

"Therefore shall a man leave his father and his mother, and shall cleave unto his wife: and they shall be one flesh" (Gen. 2:24). God established the family.

"Then they that gladly received his word were baptized: and the same day there were added unto them about three thousand souls. And they continued steadfastly in the apostles' doctrine and fellowship, and in breaking of bread, and in prayer" (Acts 2:41). God established the church later.

God honored this decision of mine; for as I stayed home more with Ken, showing him that he came first in my life after God, he began to willingly attend church activities more often. This was about the time we began to share the Bible study together. To this day, I have carefully considered my priorities; and I have a devout Christian for a husband.

There is one other lesson of importance I have learned from my experience as an overzealous Christian. I have learned that the desire to teach is usually strong, but the ability to convey God's message is ineffective. The apostle Paul spent a time of preparation in Arabia, learning from the Holy Spirit before he attempted to begin his real ministry.[4]

So many of our churches are careless in their choice of Sunday School or Bible study teachers. Due to teacher shortages, they are often only too happy and relieved to make use of untrained volunteers. This was true in my case, and I found myself teaching a class of intelligent and knowledgeable fifth- and sixth-grade children, who knew more about the Bible than I did. I could convey to them a zeal for the Lord, but I could not answer many of their questions. Many times I resorted to planned sessions which dealt with God's goodness and power but very little of God's Word. I was distinctly embarrassed during one session when an astute boy clearly showed me to be in error.

"The Wise Men came to see the baby Jesus in the manger," I said, during a class just preceding Christmas, "and bowed down and worshiped Him."

"No, Mrs. Beavers," countered this star pupil. "The Wise Men came to see the boy Jesus when He was around two years old. It says so in the Book of Luke, right near the beginning."

Sure enough, it was there in chapter 2! I believe a look in the mirror on my part would have revealed a deep-pink complexion!

I soon realized I was not teacher material, and I did not teach again until I was much further grounded in the Word of God. It is bad enough to be embarrassed by one's own students, but it is indeed worse to mislead them due to lack of knowledge. If we are to follow the apostle Paul's admonition to Timothy, "Study to shew thyself approved unto God, a workman that needeth not to be ashamed, rightly dividing the word of truth" (2

Tim. 2:15), we must first of all *know* the Word in full context before we teach it to others.

In summary, prevention of witness overkill involves presenting a loving witness. Pressure tactics must be avoided like the plague.

Any feeling of self-righteousness must be taken to the foot of the cross and left there, replacing it with a mantle of humility and gratitude for the blessing God has so graciously given you. Be especially sensitive to the feelings of the person to whom you have chosen to witness. Feel out his or her spiritual needs with such possible questions as: "What church do you attend?"

If the answer indicates a church, you might add, "Are your needs being met there?" Often this will open up a possibility for a witness on your part.

If the answer is, "I don't attend any church," you have an opportunity to extend an invitation to your own church. In either case, this might be the time to share your testimony with that person, telling him or her what God has done in your life.

Be especially careful in discussing your spiritual gift or gifts with the non-Christian. This has no place in a winsome, loving witness.

If you are a new Christian with a special zeal for God, make certain your priorities are in order before trying to evangelize "the world." God does not want us to neglect our own—even for His sake —for He does give us our wives, husbands, and children to care for and nurture.

It is extremely difficult to use teaching as a witness tool until we are sufficiently grounded in the Word of God. To do otherwise is to tread on very dangerous ground.

In order to become a fruitful witness for Jesus Christ, first pray for the guidance of the Holy Spirit, tell what Jesus has done in your own life, and remember to be winsome in order to win some. Then let God do His work in the other person.

"He that winneth souls is wise" (Prov. 11:30).

"The heart of the wise teacheth his mouth, and addeth learning to his lips" (Prov. 16:23).

Epilogue

The insights about which I have written have been put to the test the last few years. The views I have shared have also been strengthened as a result of experience. I am not trying to say I have reached the goal I have been seeking—that of being ". . . approved unto God" (2 Tim. 2:15), but Ken and I have been given some great opportunities to plant seeds and lead a few people to Christ. This was not done on our own, of course. God, through the Holy Spirit, has enabled these things to happen, and we are humbly grateful to have been instruments of sorts.

One of these opportunities came when Evangelist Billy Graham scheduled a crusade here in Tallahassee. This was the result of the prayers of many people over a period of seven years. Work on the crusade began about a year before it was to take place, and the excitement and anticipation gained momentum monthly, weekly, and then daily.

I had the distinct privilege of taking part in these

plans in two ways. Prayer "triplets" were formed all over the area of North Florida, South Georgia, and parts of Alabama. Each prayer triplet—three people meeting for prayer—met once a week at a designated place to pray for nine people they wanted to be affected by the crusade.

From this alone, wonderful things began to happen to the community. Some people began attending church long before the crusade. Some had spiritual and physical healings. When the crusade began, many of these people did attend, not just once, but several nights. Many committed their lives to Christ.

"Mom, I'm coming home," were the words heard over long-distance telephone by a tearful and grateful mother whose son had left home about two years previous and had not been heard from. The years of prayer by the parents were now being answered.

I personally had the hearing in my left ear miraculously restored, through no prayer effort on the part of our prayer triplet. I had long accepted my hearing loss as inevitable.

During part of this time, Billy Graham team members offered a series of courses weekly at churches all over Tallahassee. I attended one of these and was richly blessed by the inspirational and instructional material. We were given opportunities to practice what we had learned on others present, and this served to provide a measure of

confidence where many of us felt inadequate to
the task ahead. We were to be counselors at the
crusade, and none of us knew what situation we
would encounter.

"Speak in love," was a clear admonition to each
of us who were to pair up with one of the persons
who responded to the evangelist's invitation at the
end of a service. We were not to adopt a "holier-
than-thou" attitude; but instead, we were to in-
troduce ourselves to the person, find out exactly
why the person came forward, and proceed according to his or her need.

We learned that there are many reasons why
people come forward at a crusade, and that it is
extremely important to know the motive behind
each one.

It is estimated that about 50 percent come forward to make a decision for Christ. After the initial
introductions, the counselor asks the inquirer
(term used for person coming forward) if he or she
desires to make a commitment; and after a "yes"
answer, certain Bible Scriptures are shared and
explained in a manner easily understood. The two
then pray together, with the inquirer repeating
the words after they are said by the counselor. This
is helpful for people who do not pray easily. It is
then a time for rejoicing and assurance that the
inquirer is now in the kingdom of God, a child of
God, with the knowledge that he or she will be
with God throughout eternity. More important

than the words spoken is what is in the heart that counts. If this desire for commitment were not in the inquirer's heart, he or she would probably not have come forward in the first place. It is not a matter of head knowledge or simply mouthing words, but it is the acknowledgment of Christ publicly: "Whosoever shall confess me before men, him shall the Son of man also confess before the angels of God" (Luke 12:8).

We learned that many people come forward for other reasons; and perhaps one of the most unusual was that an inquirer desired the autograph of Billy Graham. Fortunately, this is not the normal reason! Some want assurance of salvation, even though a commitment has been made previously. This assurance is easily given by such verses of Scripture as:

> My sheep hear my voice, and I know them, and they follow me: And I give unto them eternal life: and they shall never perish, neither shall any man pluck them out of my hand. My Father which gave them me, is greater than all; and no man is able to pluck them out of my Father's hand (John 10:27-29).

Some people come forward to seek forgiveness and restoration of fellowship with God. These are people who have received Christ but have failed Him in some way, and are now seeking forgiveness. In this case, the counselor would refrain from asking about any sin but would quote from the Bible: "If we confess our sins, he is faithful and just to forgive us our sins, and to cleanse us from all righteousness" (1 John 1:9). It is important to disclose to the person that we not only confess our sins and forsake them, but we are also to make things right—if at all possible—with those whom we have wronged.

When I was a teenager it was a fad to take home a dessert spoon from a well-known hotel when attending a dinner dance there. When I became a Christian, I had two such silver-plated dessert spoons in my possession, almost forty years later! Soon my conscience began to prick me, and I placed each spoon in a box and mailed them back to the respective hotels in Chicago and Fort Worth. As long as I held them, I was a thief; but now I had asked God's forgiveness, and the wrong was righted, I hoped. I didn't know whether the old Chicago hotel even existed when I mailed the package; but as I sat beside a dear elderly lady at a luncheon following my trip to the post office, we began to speak of something we found in common: we had both lived in Chicago. Right out of the blue, she asked me: "Did you know that the Drake Hotel is erecting a new building?"

My question was answered. One of the spoons I had mailed was to the Drake Hotel in Chicago.

Some people are unsure of their own relation-

ship to Christ. The basic question to ask that person
is whether or not there had been a time in his or
her life when he or she had made a definite commitment to Christ as Lord and Savior. If a "yes"
answer is given, then the same words can be used
as are used with those needing assurance of salvation. If a "no" answer is given, the same words can
be used as are used with those seeking salvation.

In the case of a doubtful or vague answer, the
Evangelism Explosion initial question can be
asked: "If you were to die tonight, do you know for
certain that you will go to heaven?" If there are
still doubts, then the counselor can share the Scriptures which show the person how he can find salvation.

Let me simply suggest some excellent witness-
ing materials and programs. *Continuing Witness
Training* is available from the Home Mission
Board, Southern Baptist Convention, 1350 Spring
Street NW, Atlanta, Georgia 30309. CWT is a thir-
teen-week course usually conducted by an espe-
cially trained pastor or layperson. *WIN* is a
program and materials prepared by the Church
Training Department, Baptist Sunday School
Board, Nashville, Tennessee. The materials may be
ordered from the Materials Services Department,
BSSB, 127 Ninth Avenue North, Nashville,
Tennessee 37234.

In witnessing, it is always best to close the conversation with prayer and urge the person to read

and study the Bible and hopefully to join a Bible study group. If the person does not attend a church, an invitation to your own church would always be in order; but it may be more helpful to assist the person in finding a church near their home.

For more detailed information on witnessing, I recommend *The Billy Graham Christian Worker's Handbook*, published by World Wide Publications in Minneapolis, Minnesota.

The more difficult type of witnessing (at least to me) is where the "stage" is not set—witnessing on a one-to-one basis. We want others to know Christ as we do, but how do we go about introducing the subject and then following through with it? Close family and friends are the formidable ones to approach. They have known us and our weaknesses for a long time. They often doubt what we are saying is real. They do not desire us to suggest any change in their lives, especially if their lives are fairly comfortable. It is as Jesus said, "A prophet is not without honour, save in his own country, and in his own house" (Matt. 13:57*b*). I am certainly not trying in any way to compare myself or others with having the role of a prophet, but it is a similar situation. We have news to proclaim, but those closest to us resent what we are saying and refuse to listen. We are still simply "Aunt So-and-so" or "Uncle What's-his-name" to them. And, of course, this is true.

Isaiah's prophecy speaks well to this issue:

> You will be ever hearing but never understand-
> ing;
> You will be ever seeing but never perceiving.
> For this people's heart has become calloused;
>   they hardly hear with their ears,
>   and they have closed their eyes.[1]
> Otherwise they might see with their eyes,
>   hear with their ears,
>   understand with their hearts
> and turn, and I would heal them (Isa. 6:9-10, NIV).

Sometimes, however, opportunities arise which we must respond to if we are to be obedient to God. One such opportunity came to Ken and me one time when a distraught father sought us out and told us his son was about to leave college and the area to do work for the church to which he belonged. It would mean that his schooling would be interrupted for approximately two years, and the father felt that he would essentially be wasting two years of his life. The church was obviously not Christian. It was an excellent counterfeit, and no amount of persuasion or reason would change the young man's mind. The parents were up against a solid wall.

Ken and I were mere acquaintances of the young man—not close friends. We asked if we might come over to see him, and he agreed. The parents told him why we would be coming; and for some reason, he was willing to talk with us. We spoke to him lovingly and told him some of the things we knew about his religion and compared them with the Bible. We had made a study of various religions and cults over a long period of time, much of which we learned in the Bible course we had taken together and which I mentioned in chapter 6 of this book. We had also known quite a number of people of various religious convictions, especially the one this young man was in. We were low key in all that we said, and we did not put him down or judge him. Neither did we tell him what to do. But something must have made an impression, for he so informed us later.

We went away on a trip soon after our encounter; and when we returned and attended church the following Sunday, we had a greeting such as we had rarely received before.

"Guess who's out of 'such and such' church!" the excited father all but shouted. And then he pointed to his grinning son, who generously hugged us and stammered out his new joy. It seems that he had been challenged by his father to seek out certain information in the library, not just take his own word for it. The young man complied and came home angry and resentful.

"I've been duped!" he proclaimed to his family. "I'm getting out of that church!"

And he did. Best of all, he turned to the church of his family, a church which proclaimed Jesus

Christ as Lord. He works there with the young people to the day of my writing this chapter, and he is helping them to build a solid spiritual foundation based upon the Bible.

One day I was given the sad news that a dear neighbor of ours was in the hospital with a very serious illness, with little chance of recovery. I called her on the phone, after being told that she would welcome such a call.

"Please come and see me," she entreated. "I want to get my life straightened out."

I knew what she meant by these words, as I had attempted to witness to her about Christ on several occasions—always with the answer that she was not quite ready. Now it appeared that she was ready.

I all but trembled when I entered her room, for fear that I would not say the right thing. However, I had taken a friend with me to stay outside the room and pray for me; and, of course, I sent up a plea for help from above before I went in to see her.

I was shocked at her appearance—the weight loss, the pallor, and the glassy expression in her eyes. But she smiled and indicated she was happy that I had come. She looked, and was, very weary, so I came to the point quite soon. She was ready to hear what I had to say, and I gently told her that Jesus loved her. I quoted some Scriptures and told her how the Bible says we can have eternal life.

"Do you want to accept Jesus as your Lord and Savior now?" I asked.

"Yes, I do," she replied.

I prayed, and she repeated the words after me.

"Did you mean what you said?" I inquired.

"Yes, I did," she affirmed.

"You are now a child of God," I assured her, "and you will have eternal life. The Bible gives us this confidence."

"It sounds almost too easy," she confessed.

"It *is* easy," I conceded. "Salvation is not given by what we do but by what we believe in our hearts. If we commit our lives to Jesus Christ, yield our lives to Him, and repent of our sins, we do have salvation—salvation from sin and from eternal separation from God. We obey Him because He sends the Holy Spirit to guide us and direct our ways. We also obey Him because of our love for Him."

She thought for a moment and then said, "I feel so much better now."

It was a time of rejoicing for us and for her family.

There are really no pat rules for what to say to others in witnessing for Christ. Each situation and need is different, and it is necessary to identify with each person and try to have empathy with him or her. It is necessary to find out where each person is coming from and to respond to that person in love and understanding. It is most important to be the person's friend and reach out to him or her as any friend would.

I have found that one of the worst things we can do is be judgmental. All we have to do is look deeply into our own hearts, and there is always sin which needs confessing. But one thing we know: "If we confess our sins, he is faithful and just to forgive us our sins, and to cleanse us from all unrighteousness" (1 John 1:9).

The utmost in witnessing to others is to live our own lives in a way that is without reproach. I am not speaking about being self-righteous. I am speaking more of the love we show others. I am speaking of putting the needs of others above our own selfish desires. There is something insincere about the Christian who proclaims a great love for others but has no time to show it. There is something insincere about the Christian who spends his money on himself or herself but does not give to the needy.

I feel it is a form of showing our love for others by being a good driver, by being courteous to salespersons, by saying "thank you," "please," and "I appreciate your help." We can show our love by sharing joy and laughter. There are countless ways of saying, "I care for you."

"A child is more likely to see God as Father if he sees God in his own father. . . . Children need models more than they need critics."[2]

That is witnessing in its finest form.

Notes

Chapter 2
1. A. W. Tozer, *When He Is Come* (Harrisburg, Penn.: Christian Publications, Inc., 1968), p. 94.

Chapter 6
1. Sam Shoemaker, *Under New Management* (Grand Rapids: Zondervan Publishing House, 1966), p. 90.
2. Ibid., p. 93.
3. Colleen Townsend Evans, *A New Joy* (New York: n.d.), p. 26.
4. James I. Packer, et al, *The Bible Almanac* (Nashville: Thomas Nelson, Publishers, 1980), p. 552.

Epilogue
1. See marginal note in HOLY BIBLE *New International Version*, Isaiah 6:9-10, Hebrew; Septuagint.
2. "Our Daily Bread," Radio Bible Class. June, July, August, 1986, Grand Rapids, Mich.